LLC

QuickStart Guide

The Simplified Beginner's Guide to Limited Liability Companies

ClydeBank BUSINESS

Edition # 1 – Updated : April 13, 2016

Cover Illustration and Design: Katie Poorman, Copyright © 2016 by ClydeBank Media LLC
Interior Design: Katie Poorman, Copyright © 2016 by ClydeBank Media LLC

ClydeBank Media LLC
P.O Box 6561
Albany, NY 12206
Printed in the United States of America

Copyright © 2016
ClydeBank Media LLC
www.clydebankmedia.com
All Rights Reserved

ISBN-13 : 978-0996366762

contents

Terms displayed in **_bold italic_** can be found
defined in the glossary, starting on page 71.
&
Feel free to take notes beginning on page 76.

introduction

LLCs (Limited Liability Companies) are becoming increasingly popular. Aspiring entrepreneurs and small business owners catch wind of them, learn that they can be used to limit their personal liabilities in the event of a major business disaster and think, "Hmmm, this almost sounds like a free form of business loss insurance..." and, to some extent, they're right.

While an LLC offers tremendous advantages as a structure for businesses, understanding the appropriate steps to take in starting one and what's really transpiring, in a legal sense, can require a lot of explaining. The intent of this book is to provide a sound understanding of how an LLC is formed, how it operates, and how it can be leveraged for the greatest benefit for your small business.

You may be wondering if a book and a little Internet research will adequately prepare you for setting up your LLC. Here's the deal: LLCs are a relatively new type of business structure. In fact, the first LLC was started less than 40 years ago in Wyoming. It was introduced as a mechanism to remedy what were perceived as shortcomings in other business structure formats, and the void it fills—in the business sense—is often a benefit to those who elect to take advantage of the LLC format.

The idea of the LLC caught on, and by the 1990s LLCs could be formed in every state. That's the other thing about LLCs: they're formed within the state. You can't just go into business at-will, as you would with a sole proprietorship or a partnership. You have to file Articles of Organization in the state of your choice. We'll talk more about how to choose the right state for your LLC in Chapter 6. The basics of the LLC are similar from state to state, but not identical. We're going to cover the the more universal elements of LLCs, while being sure to direct you towards resoucres with more state-specific information.

| 1 |

LLC Basics

Do I Need A Lawyer?

Since the LLC is a newer form of business entity, there's still a lot to be decided by the courts when it comes to how LLCs operate under the law. So, the safest answer to this question is "yes", but, as you can probably infer, that's also the most expensive option. With each passing year, and as more and more case law is generated that helps us understand the role of LLCs in the business environment, it's become easier and easier to do things on your own. We're living in an age in which it's easy to find great books (like this one!) and sophisticated online tools (such as legalzoom.com [no affiliation]). These inexpensive and at times free resources may provide sufficient information for certain individuals in certain states. Other individuals may find that the best option is to hire an attorney to help walk them through the process of forming an LLC.

Pass-Through Taxation

If you don't already understand the concept of 'pass-through taxation', then it is a good idea to get your head around it before you delve too deeply into this analysis of LLCs. Pass-through taxation refers to the taxing of business income through the taxing of personal income. It's one of the fundamental factors that distinguishes LLCs and sole proprietorships from corporations; LLCs and sole proprietorships are subject to pass-through taxation. The business entity itself isn't taxed, but the business earnings are taxed as part of the owner's individual personal income.

*Note : When business income is taxed via pass-through taxation, the business entity itself is classified by the IRS as a **disregarded entity**, meaning, an entity that exists but is not directly taxed.*

Pass-through taxation isn't necessarily a bad thing, but it can definitely be more expensive than corporate taxation. In fact, whenever you ask your lawyer to review the negatives of the LLC model, this usually tops the list. Here's why: when a corporation's profits are taxed, Medicare and Social Security taxes aren't imposed (1.45% and 6.2%, respectively). For corporations, these types of taxes are only imposed on the salaries the corporation pays to its employees. When a person is acting as a sole proprietor, or when a group of people is acting as an LLC, their business profit is subject to Medicare and Social Security, as well as standard federal, state and local taxes. Pass-through taxation operates just like *self-employment tax*, so the LLC owner or partner is paying the full portion of his Social Security and Medicare obligations in taxes, as opposed to splitting these tax burdens with his employer.

Note : Ordinarily, when an individual is working for an employer, the employer pays 50% of the federally-required Medicare and Social Security withholdings. When an individual is classified as self-employed, he or she is responsible for paying 100% of the federal withholding. This Social Security funding tax is known as SECA, instead of FICA—Self Employed Contributions Act and Federal Insurance Contributions Act, respectively. The good news for small business owners is that your 'employer' portion of the SECA tax (50%) can be written off.

It's important to point out here that LLCs can opt to be taxed as corporations. We'll go into further detail on taxation in Chapter 5.

Other Potential Disadvantages to an LLC

One of the problems with the general public's current understanding of LLCs is that they're not all that clear on the downsides. Why stick with a sole proprietorship or a partnership when you can be absolved from all debt and legal liability with an LLC? In some ways it really is true, even though it may seem too good to be true. LLCs are awesome!

When you form an LLC, you and your co-founders or co-owners will only put at risk the money and the financial assets that you contribute to the LLC. If the LLC gets into trouble and can't pay its debts, or if someone wages a lawsuit against your LLC and wins, then they're not going to get your house, your car, or anything out of your personal bank account.

What this means for you is if you have very little money in the bank, what you don't put into your business is protected. On the other hand, if you've got a lot of assets, a high net worth, etc., and you want to open up a construction company, then you should seriously consider going with an LLC to keep your personal assets safe in the event of an on-the-job accident or some other unforeseen event that ends up exerting a serious financial burden on your business. Many view this as a win-win situation. Every business person understands that he shouldn't invest more that he is willing to lose, and an LLC essentially guarantees that what he elects not to invest stays safe.

If you're just looking to devote yourself to the humble but delicious pursuit of being a donut shop owner, you could go the LLC route, but getting started is going to be a lot more time consuming and expensive. This is the chief setback of the LLC structure; when starting a sole proprietorship, you can pretty much just get up and go into business. You'll have to make sure you have the proper licensure and permits, and you'll need to keep track of your earnings for tax purposes, but that's really about it.

When you take the LLC route, things aren't so simple. You have to register in your state. You must form your articles of organization (more on that in Chapter 3); you need to pay a filing fee, which is usually several hundred dollars, and you're more likely to require the services of an attorney, especially if multiple individuals are going to be involved in the LLC.

This brings us to the next major disadvantage of the LLC model: the lack of clearly defined roles. LLC owners often need attorneys to help create a legally binding framework for the "who's responsible and for what" and "who's allowed to do what and when" aspects of an LLC. In short, once you've gotten your business plan and your organizational chart together, an LLC doesn't automatically provide the legal framework for such company particulars as who is in charge of which portion of your operations.

Such role definition is much more sorely needed when forming an LLC than when forming a corporation. Corporations have a useable organizational structure built into the paperwork, and their legal responsibilities and authorizations already come pre-defined. You have a board of directors, a chairman, officers, shareholders, and so on. Everyone knows his or her role. This is not the case at all when forming an LLC.

Note : Luckily, there's a workaround for this problem in the form of an "LLC Operating Agreement," a legally binding document that defines ownership roles, authorizations, and profit-shares in an LLC.

Some states (a minority) require LLC Operating Agreements, but they're generally good to have for most any newly formed LLC. Do you need a lawyer to form one? Again, this is a question that has to be answered on a case-by-case basis. Some of the relevant factors to consider: how complex is your agreement going to be, and how well do you trust the people with whom you're going into business?

Another potential downside for the LLC is the difficulty in transferring ownership. Unfortunately, if you're a co-owner in an LLC, you can't just give away or sell your shares in the endeavor. You're limited to 'assigning' your interests over to another party. The legal process of assignment is fairly straightforward, though it is more complicated than simply signing a sheet of paper. Assignment means that the person to whom you assign your interests—the assignee—will have the right to receive all the profits that you would normally have received through your ownership in the LLC.

The assignee *does not* automatically get your voting rights or operational control. In order for the assignee to have operational control, the other members must vote in a majority. It's really quite simple in most cases, but if the rest of your LLC ownership doesn't want the assignee to have any control over the company, then there's nothing you can do. There are even some jurisdictions where, if an owner departs the LLC, then the enterprise legally ceases to exist and an entirely new organization must be formed. Individuals forming LLCs in these jurisdictions need to refine their operating agreements to account for prospective member departures.

These problems with ownership transfer extend into other dimensions of LLC operation and growth as well. For example, it's very difficult to take an LLC public because that would involve diffusing ownership to shareholders, and since ownership isn't easily transferable, most LLCs do not end up going public. Furthermore, because of this restriction, certain venture capitalists with an eye for taking companies public won't be willing to open up their pockets for you.

The bottom line is that before you choose to form an LLC, you should have a clear exit strategy for your business so you don't get stuck in a situation in which your business wants to expand or change in a certain way but your legal structure confines it, like a small garden pot holding a plant that wants to spread its roots or branches but can't.

In Chapter 7 we'll cover converting LLCs into different entity types, such as corporations. Such a conversion can be extremely expensive and taxed to the nth degree, but that may be the price you have to pay for not planning your exit strategy.

Focus on the Positives

Despite the concerns, there are a lot of positives to forming an LLC, especially as opposed to a sole proprietorship.

Flexibility in Profit Distribution

Unlike corporations in which profit share is legally mandated to reflect the percentage of shareholder interest, LLCs have a distinct flexibility of profit distribution. For example, if Bob owns 25% of Corporation X, then Bob may receive no more or no less than 25% of Corporation X's profit distributions. With LLCs, though there is a legal basis for who's entitled to the profits—the amount of contribution they have contributed thus far—over time it's ultimately left to the discretion of the members to distribute profit as they please.

Flexible Tax Status

LLCs are the only entities permitted to choose their own tax status. By default, they are taxed as partnerships, which means that profits and losses are passed on to the owners via the pass-through taxation structure. LLC owners wishing to change their taxation method can do so by filing *Form 8832* with the IRS. Once this form is filed, however, the LLC will be stuck with that status for five years, so think it over before you commit to a change.

> *Note : The tax flexibility afforded an LLC can be used to make sound strategic business decisions. The tax method elected in Form 8832 can be retroactively applied to the business for up to a year (sometimes as much as three years depending on the jurisdiction). This means that you can have your accountant evaluate how your business would fare under multiple tax systems before choosing how you want to be taxed.*

Losses Can Be Split

With an LLC, a business' losses can be distributed between its owners in any way they see fit. The losses written off by a member on his tax return do not have to be proportionate to that member's ownership percentage. Therefore, if one of the LLC firm members, for instance, were to purchase a very expensive piece of equipment using his own credit card without being reimbursed by the company, then he would be allowed to write off the whole of that loss on his tax return, regardless of how much formal ownership he had in the LLC.

LLCs in Action: The Hawkeye Agricultural Consultancy

Jonathan owns a repair garage in Ottumwa, Iowa that specializes in motorized agricultural equipment repairs. Jonathan's friend, Larry, has worked on a nearby farm for most of his life and understands the essentials of agriculture. He knows when to plant various crops, how to care for them and when to harvest them. Their mutual acquaintance, Jim Bob, is the manager of a major distributorship of popular and reliable tractors.

One evening over a pint of moonshine (legal moonshine of course), the three of them come up with an idea: The Hawkeye Agricultural Consultancy. They're going to pool their resources and skills and offer to manage farmland for absentee landlords and retirees; essentially, anyone who wants to own and profit from farm land but doesn't want to actively manage it.

They file their Articles of Organization in Iowa and come up with an Operations Agreement that suits their endeavor. Since they're going in as an LLC rather than a partnership, Jonathan's repair garage is protected. Even if their business endeavor goes tragically awry, unless Jonathan sells his garage to the LLC, he will not lose it. The LLC arrangement makes Jonathan a whole lot more comfortable with this endeavor.

The three men could have had their assets protected if they formed a corporation rather than an LLC, but all three of them find it much simpler to use their individual income tax forms to report their business incomes. With a corporation, they'd have to worry about splitting up their income from the business between what's paid to them as a salary and what's paid to the corporation as profit. If things change down the road and the LLC is generating income at levels that far exceed what the owners need to take home, then they can do the smart thing, change their LLC into a corporation, and pay the excess income directly to the corporation thereby incurring a lower tax rate (no Social Security or Medicare).

Alternatively, they could also file their Form 8832, electing to have their LLC taxed as a corporation while nominally remaining an LLC. At the end of the day their personal assets, homes, property, etc., are protected, and they have the flexibility to change their tax structure if need be.

In the following chapters, we will break down the process of deciding when to use the LLC structure and how to get your own LLC up and running.

| 2 |

Is an LLC Right for You?

The first thing you have to do when considering your emerging business is decide what kind of entity is right for your venture. Even if you hire an attorney, you can't discount the advantage of having a sound personal understanding of how your entity is going to operate.

There's no way to determine whether an LLC is a good fit unless you're aware of all your alternatives. Since the purpose of this book is to educate you on LLCs, we won't go into extensive depth on the other business entities, so please don't mistaken our scant coverage on these other business structures as a general preference for the LLC structure. Depending on the circumstances that surround your business, any one of these structures may offer the optimum fit. The advantages and disadvantages of each system of organization could fill their own books; an extensive deep dive into each alternative is beyond the scope of this book.

Sole Proprietorship

It's easy to set up a *sole proprietorship*, but the big factor to consider right off the bat is assets. When you go into business as a sole proprietor, all of your personal assets suddenly belong to the business, meaning, if the business is ordered to pay a certain amount in a legal settlement or to clear an incurred debt, then the personal wealth you've accumulated over your lifetime must be used, if need be, to clear these obligations.

The major advantage of the sole-proprietorship is, of course, the ease with which it can be established. For example, consider a fictitious sole proprietor named Bill. Bill has just graduated from college and has known for some time that he doesn't want a job in corporate America, clawing his way up the hierarchy while working for someone else. Bill wants to be an entrepreneur. Bill gets his first big idea at age 22. He's going to start a tour company in Washington, DC, but it won't be just any tour company. *Segway through the Capital* is Bill's entrepreneurial creation, a tour company that ushers visitors through the city by way of awkward two-wheeled stand-up vehicles known as Segways. Bill knows he's sitting on a serious hit and he jumps right in, gets his marketing plan together, figures out his costs, and enlists help where needed.

Now, Bill is fresh out of school with no serious assets. Once he acquires his fleet of Segways, they will be his proprietorship's most valued assets and will be the first to be liquidated should Bill fall upon unfortunate times. Even though Bill is a sole proprietor, he's still fairly well insulated from any catastrophic scenario involving the forfeiture of personal assets. If someone falls and breaks his neck during one of Bill's tours, and Bill forgot to have him sign a waiver beforehand, the absolute worst scenario that Bill faces is losing his business and whatever personal assets he's acquired, such as a car. Even though this isn't a very cheery situation for Bill, it's still a lot better than losing his house or a huge accumulation of personal liquid assets as a result of bad business fortune.

Perhaps once Bill's Segway business starts to take off and he begins opening up shop in different cities and his net worth increases, then it will be time to convert his sole proprietorship into an LLC. At such a time, he'll likely have the money to do so. There are some other drawbacks to the sole proprietorship model.

Financing Difficulty

If you're looking to raise capital from outside sources, then you're going to have some trouble, as you can't sell off equity in a sole proprietorship the same way you can with an LLC, corporation, or even a partnership. Your capital options are limited mostly to debt capital and grants.

Finite Enterprise Longevity

When you form a corporation or LLC, the entity is essentially infinite and will continue to run so long as there are interested and invested parties available to run it; this condition persists even long after you're gone. With a sole proprietorship, once you die, that's it. Your assets are put through probate (or 'surrogate court' as it is called in some jurisdictions) and possibly sold off.

No New Credit Lines

If you're willing to get all your DBA (Doing Business As) documentation together, you can open up a checking account using the name of your business, i.e. Segway Through The Capital. The problem arises if you're still technically a sole proprietor, because you will not be able to obtain separate credit lines for your business the way you would if your business were an LLC or corporation. You will need to rely on your own credit to finance your business.

Partnership

When comparing *partnerships* to LLCs, the points of comparison are extremely similar to those used when comparing sole proprietorships to LLCs. Think of partnerships as *joint* sole proprietorships. Two people go into business together and essentially agree to be co-sole proprietors.

Partnerships can be just as easy to initiate as sole proprietorships. There's no paperwork that you're required to legally file in order to be a recognized business entity. You simply have to start doing business with someone else (or with multiple other people as partnerships are not limited to two people) who agree to share the profits and losses. Partnerships can begin without any formal documentation; a handshake or verbal agreement will suffice.

The problem arises if you fail to get something down in writing, because you'll be at the mercy of your state's one-size-fits-all laws that govern partnerships. Usually, things are kept pretty simple. Profits are to be split right down the middle or in accordance with each partner's capital contributions. This could be a simple 'every partner has an equal share' agreement, or it could be staggered to represent each partner's level of financial commitment.

Just as is in a sole proprietorship, all members in a partnership can be held personally liable for debts and legal judgments incurred by the company. Let's say that a guy named Ben and a guy named Jerry want to go into the frozen yogurt business. Jerry's net worth is considerable. He owns two houses, a boat, and a rare collection of ancient Chinese artifacts that he won in a poker game in Thailand.

Ben, on the other hand, though a whiz at making frozen yogurt, doesn't really have a lot going on in the asset department. He rents his house and drives an old beat-up '84 Datsun. So Ben and Jerry rent a storefront in a strip mall and get all the equipment they need to start selling frozen yogurt. Months go by and hardly a single customer wanders into their store. They owe rent, they still owe for the equipment they're leasing, and they have a modest payroll to meet. The sales from the yogurt shop can cover about 10% of their debt.

Since Ben and Jerry are partners, their creditors can go after either one of them for repayment of the whole amount of their company debt. In other words, if the vendor of the SaniServ Frozen Yogurt machine, who's been leasing his equipment to Ben and Jerry for four months, can only get his money back from Jerry, rather than Ben, then he's entitled to go after Jerry for the full amount. If Ben is less than forthcoming with his share, Jerry can sue Ben for his share of the liability, assuming he's willing to pay all the associated legal fees that such a pursuit would require.

In the case of Ben and Jerry, Jerry should have insisted on forming an LLC or a corporation *before* going into business with Ben to avoid this very scenario.

Corporations

As defined by late 19th century satirist, Ambrose Bierce, a corporation is "an ingenious device for obtaining profit without individual responsibility." Though less than complimentary, Bierce touches on the entire point of incorporation.

Corporations, much more so than partnerships and sole proprietorships, have strong similarities to LLCs. They are both governed by the state and require filing and fees to be recognized—articles of incorporation or **articles of organization** for corporations and LLCs respectively. Secondly, and most importantly, these entities insulate their members from putting their personal assets at risk from liabilities incurred by the company.

Here's another interesting quotation from a more contemporary figure: politician Mitt Romney, who was the Republican candidate for president of the U.S. in 2012. "Corporations are people, my friend." Romney delivered this line in a town hall meeting in Iowa, and even though he was heavily criticized for such a pronouncement, he was actually right, at least in a legal sense.

Corporations are distinct from all other types of business entities because they are recognized by federal and state laws as "legal persons." Corporations can enter into contracts with other corporations or persons. Corporations can incur debts and be issued credit. Corporations can even purchase ownership shares in LLCs. Most interestingly, and perhaps most disturbingly, as of the *Citizens United v. Federal Election Commission* Supreme Court decision in 2011, Corporations have essentially unlimited freedom of speech, protected by the constitution.

Corporations come in two primary forms, *C corporations*—named for Subchapter C of the Internal Revenue Code—and *S corporations*, named for Subchapter S. C corporations are the most standard version of this business entity, while S corporations are entities that begin as C Corporations but later elect to be subject to a pass-through taxation, the same style of taxation used by sole proprietorships and partnerships. When a corporation files to be an S corporation, it is strictly a tax adjustment, not a legal status adjustment. Though the entity will be taxed differently, it retains the same abilities and obligations of a standard C corporation.

One of the most important and fundamental differences between corporations and LLCs is in the transferability of ownership. You'll notice that publicly-traded companies are all corporations. This is because they must have the flexibility to be bought and sold in the form of shares, or stock. Another key difference is that, unlike LLCs, corporations have been around for a long, long time. The Ambrose Bierce quotation from the beginning of this section is from well over a hundred years ago. The first corporation ever to exist is commonly thought to be Britain's East India Tea Company that was founded in approximately the year 1600.

The point is that there's been an awful lot of time for the corporate structure to be 'tried on' by the business world. A billion and one different questions have arisen. A billion and one different disputes have also arisen and been adjudicated. As a result, the case law governing the use of the term corporation, not to mention the behavior and responsibilities of corporations is very robust to say the least. LLCs, on the other hand, are brand new by comparison, and the laws and customs that surround them are still nascent. In situations in which there are no clear laws on the books, then "we have to make it up as we go."

Another implication of the relative paucity of case law surrounding LLCs is that there are not as many record-keeping requirements as there are with corporations. In a corporation, for example, in order to protect your personal assets and maintain the corporation's "personhood" status, regular meetings have to be set up involving specific parties such as the board of directors, the corporation's officers, as well as shareholders. Failure to demonstrate evidence that these meetings took place can result in the *piercing of the corporate veil*, which puts the personal assets of the corporation's shareholders/owners at risk.

While LLCs don't have quite so many formal record keeping requirements, neither do they have as much case law on the books explicitly stating when meetings are not necessary. Corporations at least have the luxury of knowing with a great deal of clarity what's expected of them. LLCs are more inclined to finding themselves at the mercy of a novel situation.

An interesting factoid about LLCs, and another distinction point separating the LLC/corporation entities, is that LLCs have what's called ***dual protection*** for their owners while corporations cannot offer the same for their shareholders.

If your grandmother, over the course of her life, has invested steadily in stocks—mostly mining stocks, a few utilities, and some shares in a big pharmaceutical company—and the pharmaceutical company gets into some trouble and has to settle a massive class action lawsuit, no one's going to come after your grandmother's home, even if the drug company goes belly up because of this awful lawsuit. But what about a reversed scenario?

What if your grandmother is found to be personally liable for something else, something completely unrelated to her stock portfolio? Maybe she hired a man to come over and clean her gutters and let him use her ladder, which, unfortunately, turned out to be faulty. The man fell, broke three ribs and his arm, and now wants your grandmother to pay his medical bills. If granny doesn't have the cash on hand, then seizure of her stocks is fair game. Now, if your grandmother were an owner in an LLC when the gardener fell off her ladder, the gardener would not be able to seize her ownership interest in the LLC because LLCs (unlike corporations) have dual protection—protection that exists in two directions.

The taxation structure between LLCs and corporations can be different from one another, or they can be essentially the same if the LLC elects to be taxed as a corporation. We'll get into more detail on taxation in Chapter 5.

Sole Proprietorships

- High personal liability
- Easy to start, easy to run

Partnerships

- Consider them 'joint sole proprietorships'
- Easy to start, liability is shared

Corporations

- Difficult and expensive to start
- Restrictive structure and legal obligations
- Exists indefinitely

The Lesser-Known Business Entities

Some states still recognize LLPs (Limited Liability Partnerships) and LLLPs (Limited Liability Limited Partnerships). These entities were actually created before the advent of the LLC and aren't nearly as popular now because the invention of the LLC subsumes many of the benefits these lesser-known entities offer.

The LLP's primary function is to allow partnerships to be formed in which the barriers of responsibility from partner to partner are better preserved. Simply put, if an LLP is formed amongst three persons, Bob, Jane, and Roger, and Roger's actions create a liability for the business, then only Roger is responsible for attending to all repercussions resulting from the liability.

If you're looking to establish an LLC for a professional services firm, such as a group of doctors, dentists, accountants, or attorneys, then, depending on in which state you reside, you may want to take a close look at what the LLP offers you. Some states, such as California, Nevada, New York, and Oregon, limit the level of personal liability protection offered by LLCs when it comes to licensed professional services. In these states your best option will be to form an LLP.

LLLPs are offered in about half the US States and are used in ventures in which certain partners are taking an active role in managing the business while others act more as silent partners, meaning they put up a significant amount of money for the business but don't get too involved in the business's day-to-day operations. The LLLP allows for some members of the partnership (usually the silent partners) to only retain liability for their individual investment in the business, while the other members (usually the active managers) are personally liable for all debts and liabilities incurred by the business as a whole. The LLLP structure aims to provide an incentive for silent partners to invest in new business opportunities, assuming that the managing parties will perform optimally given that their personal assets are at stake.

The Most Important Considerations

Perhaps the most fundamental consideration to be made, particularly when deciding between forming an LLC or a corporation, is your long-term plan for your emerging business. If your main objective in forming a business entity is to provide a vehicle that will allow you to sensibly manage tax and liability concerns while making enough money to support yourself and your family, then an LLC is probably the right choice for you. If you're interested in a more ambitious undertaking, and your end goal is to expand the business dramatically and possibly sell it for a significant sum, then you probably want to go with the more investor-friendly entity: the corporation.

Most investors are much more comfortable investing in a corporation than they are investing in an LLC, or any entity that's taxed as a partnership. The reason for this is that most LLCs, in the early years, incur tax liability without generating a significant profit. Whatever profit is generated is usually put right back into the business during the early years of the business, and the members (in the case of an LLC), are saddled with a tax liability, even though they've not received a single dime from the company. In other words, you'd be sending your investor a tax bill before you'd be sending him or her any cash. To make matters more complicated—if the investor lives in a state outside of where the LLC operates, he or she will have technically incurred a tax liability in the state where the LLC operates and will have to file a return in that state.

> *Note : Another potential investor-related complication with LLCs: sometimes specific provisions are written into the LLC agreement that dictate the amount of profit that must be distributed to the owners, often to ensure they can pay off their tax liability. From the perspective of a business owner, this type of requirement can put limits on your flexibility in reinvesting profits back into the business.*

Corporations are generally much more attractive to investors. Despite what you might see on "business" television shows like Shark Tank, investors and venture capitalists by and large are not seeking to be partners in a business but to acquire a particular kind of capital asset that won't complicate their tax situation. Corporations meet this need by giving their initial investors a special kind of stock, referred to as "A-stock," or "preferred shares," that confer a multitude of lifelong privileges and advantages, such as anti-dilution protection, dividend payment priority, and special voting rights.

Furthermore, since there's a whole lot of case law detailing how corporations must be run when it comes to documentation, meetings, and business practices, investors take comfort knowing that a certain degree of order, organization and discipline is enforceable by law. With an LLC, there are certainly expectations to which one must adhere, but the default infrastructure isn't nearly as rigorous as it is with corporations and the result is an erosion of trust on the part of investors that makes them understandably wary of LLC-based opportunities.

Note : There are even some investors, such as venture funds, which are technically unable to invest in LLCs because they have partners who are tax exempt and are thus unable to own any company that's subject to pass-through taxation.

Finally, the general documentation used to form LLCs (Articles of Organization, etc.) tends to be more complex than the documentation used to set up corporations. Investors will thus be faced with a more intensive review process when deciding whether or not they want to invest.

| 3 |

Articles of Organization

The documentation at the heart of your LLC is your Articles of Organization. Filing these articles makes your business a legal entity that is recognized and protected by the state. Filing is done through the Secretary of State's office or whichever state office handles business registrations at you state level jurisdiction. The Articles of Organization set forth the primary identifying characteristics of your business, such as its name, owners, and the nature of the business.

Filing your Articles of Organization is your first step; it must take place before you pursue any additional filings, such as filings for various business licenses and permits. You will want to pursue these filings using the identity of your LLC, so, naturally, you will want the LLC created first. In the remainder of this chapter, we'll explore the various components of the Articles of Organization, and we'll address the age-old dilemma of whether or not you should consider hiring an attorney to help you complete this very important step in establishing your business.

Note : As with many aspects of the LLC, state laws will vary. When filing your Articles of Organization, it's important to review specific state-based requirements, which should all be available on the website of that state's business registration authority. That authority is usually the Secretary of State's Office, but not always.

The Basic Rundown

Most all forms of an LLC's Articles of Organization must include the following information, regardless of the state. In legal terminology, these information groups are referred to as 'provisions'.

The Name of the LLC

You must choose a name that's available to use in your state. When you submit your Articles of Organization, the state checks to make sure that the name is available. If it's not available, you'll be forced to resubmit your articles, often after forfeiting your initial filing fee. You should be able to conduct an independent search on the Secretary of State's (or the relevant business registration authority's) website to determine whether a name is eligible to use.

You may also want to conduct a trademark search to avoid a costly trademark infringement. This can be done on the US Patent and Trademark Office's website. A thorough discussion of trademark infringement and intellectual property law is well beyond the scope of this book; however, if you are in any way inclined to believe that trademark violation is a trifling matter, then you should probably look into learning more about trademark law.

The Purpose of the LLC

This is where you briefly state the type of business you're pursuing. Keep this section as broad as possible so that your LLC will have a maximum amount of flexibility. Some states make you specify the nitty gritty details, but most states let you keep it really broad, to the point where you can just say that the LLC's purpose is essentially limitless.

Name & Address of Your LLC's Registered Agent

Your LLC's Registered Agent is essentially the person who personifies your LLC. If someone needs to serve the LLC with legal papers, then this person is legally the person who represents the LLC and will need to be served. The Registered Agent, depending on your state, may be referred to as "Statutory Agent" or "Resident

Agent." In any event, this person and his or her address must be listed in your Articles of Organization. The Articles of Organization are public record, so, for the sake of privacy and if allowed by state law, give the office address of your registered agent rather than the home address.

Names of all the LLC's Managers & Members

All managers and members who are known at the time of filing must be listed on the Articles of Organization. It's best to have all your initial members in place at the time of filing. Though they may be changed down the road, it may, depending on the restrictions set forth in your operating agreement, be tedious to do so. Several states request that the addresses of the members and managers are also provided, so, just as with your registered agent, provide office addresses not home addresses if possible.

You may also be asked to specify the amount each member is contributing to the business in the way of money, equipment, or other capital means. In the event that you'd rather not disclose this information, or perhaps you don't even know it yet, then state what you do know or are willing to disclose, and then record the rest when you complete your Company Operating Agreement, which is not a matter of public record, free for anyone to see (see Chapter 4).

Some LLC owners are so cautious about listing various asset contributions that they elect to file their LLCs in states that don't require these unwanted disclosures. Then, they simply operate as usual and foreign-file all of their earnings, which is perfectly legal.

Here the term 'foreign' does not mean extra-national. In the business law sense the term describes a company or LLC that is subject to the laws and governance of another state. This is differentiated from 'domestic' companies, or companies that are licensed within the state and subject to that state's laws.

For example, imagine you started a trucking LLC that does business in Texas called Lone Star Trucking, but due to favorable business laws in Oklahoma you filed there instead. When operating in Texas, Lone Star Trucking is a foreign business entity. If you have offices and routes in Oklahoma, too, then your operation there is a domestic business entity. The term 'alien corporation' or 'alien entity' is used to describe an entity that fits the more traditional definition of foreign. From a business law viewpoint, alien companies are those that filed outside the US.

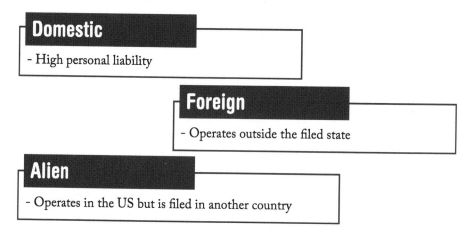

Domestic
- High personal liability

Foreign
- Operates outside the filed state

Alien
- Operates in the US but is filed in another country

Regarding Managers & Members

To clarify, managers don't necessarily have to be members, nor do members need to be managers, but, in most states, managers and members must be listed on your LLC's Articles of Organization.

Take for example, Bertram, who's interested in forming an LLC with his brother, Gary. The two of them would like to be in the electric cigarette business. They've got some money put away, and they know they can get a good rental rate on some commercial real estate that would make, in their estimation, an ideal spot for an e-cigarette or 'vaping' store.

The problem for Bertram and Gary is that they're positively put off by the whole vaping trend. They really don't want to learn the ins and outs of the business; they just want to make money from it, to cash in on a trend. So they place a job posting for a person with management experience who also has some knowledge of e-cigarettes. Once they find their manager, they will list him as such on their Articles of Organization when they form their LLC. This model for running an LLC is known as "*manager-managed*" and involves one or multiple managers looking after the business's daily operations. The manager-managed model is in contrast to the "*member-managed*" model, whereby the LLC's members (owners) also play the role of the LLC's managers.

> Note : When using the manager-managed model, be very careful when selecting whom you wish to manage the LLC. Though managers may not have ownership in the LLC, they're still permitted to unilaterally commit the business to loans, contracts and other obligations that could heavily impact the business's profitability. In simpler terms: a bad manager looking after your LLC's day-to-day operations could do a lot of damage.

Here are some things to consider when choosing member-managed or manager-managed for your LLC; *Manager-managed is better for LLCs with more members.* You want to avoid a situation in which you have too many chiefs and not enough Indians—meaning, companies function better when only one or two trusted people are authorized to make big decisions unilaterally without having to get the approval of all the LLC's members. When it comes to qualifying big decisions that can be made by management and decisions that require the full participation of the entire LLC membership, turn to the specifications you will set forth in your Operations Agreement (see Chapter 4).

Also, *be cautious and scrupulous if you're putting in a lot of your own money.* Even though the LLC structure will protect your personal assets, if you're putting in a lot of the start-up investment into the LLC, then the choice of manager becomes that much more important. Even if a member of the LLC is to be selected as a manager, you should still make sure that the selected member is going to make the most prudent decisions to protect and grow the capital that you and the other LLC members contributed.

Getting Outside Help

The best practice for protecting your investment is to focus your own energies where you excel and outsource as much as you can to other specialized parties. This argument can certainly be considered when deciding whether to draw up and file your Articles of Organization on your own or whether to hire an attorney to do it for you.

If you're forming multiple LLCs at once or converting an existing business into an LLC in which the assets of the old business must be transferred over, then you should always work with an attorney. This doesn't mean that you shouldn't consult an attorney if you're not in one of these situations, but the legal complexities of the aforementioned circumstances certainly warrant professional assistance.

Another situation that always goes smoother with an attorney in the mix is when you're selling off a large amount of ownership shares in an LLC. For this, you'll be best served by hiring, specifically, a securities attorney.

How to Find the Right Attorney

If this is the first time you've shopped for legal support, then read on. If you've gone through the process for another issue, then you can probably skip ahead to the next section, as shopping for a business counsel essentially involves the same process as shopping for any other kind of counsel.

Finding the right attorney is like finding the right house. It's delicate, very personal, and very committal. You want to find someone who's going to get to know your business from its inception (filing the

Articles of Organization) onward. You'll need someone with whom you have chemistry, someone with whom you can communicate and can trust. And, of course, you should work with someone you can afford.

Start with the good old-fashioned personal and professional network. Ask for referrals from people you and your partners know and who understand what you're trying to accomplish with your business. If you're not yet traveling in social business circles, then begin by going online and taking a peek around at various legal listings and business community forums.

As a best practice, contact attorneys whose focus is narrower. You want someone who handles the formation of LLCs and other related business matters on a day-to-day basis. Don't take meetings with attorneys if you have doubts or serious reservations, as they could likely charge you a couple hundred dollars just to waste your time for an hour. For pricing, expect at least $1,000 to set up your LLC with an attorney's help. Interested in something not quite so expensive? You could always try a *formation company*.

Formation Companies

Formation companies are among the business-related phenomena born of the Internet age, though not all formation companies are exclusively Internet-based. They are specialized outfits whose business revolves around the continual formation of LLCs and other businesses, while also offering various other streamlined legal services. The upside to using a formation company is the price. Rather than $1000, you're looking at only a few hundred dollars to set up your LLC, or possibly as little as $99. The other piece of good news is that formation companies, because of their ongoing experience setting up LLCs, are quite proficient at what they do. Most of them even have relationships with various states' Secretary of State offices, which allows them to process your formation much quicker than you could have on your own.

Formation companies can be quite useful, just be sure that you find a good one. Since they began to first show up on the business scene in 2001, formation companies have sprouted up by the truckload, and many are subpar.

Some things to consider when shopping for a formation company:

- Customer reviews

- Does the formation company know its way around the LLC formation process in all 50 states or at least in the state(s) relevant to you?

- Does the formation company have attorneys and accountants on staff to provide customized advice if need be? Does this advice end when the formation is over, or will the formation company offer support down the road as well?

Additional Provisions

You may add provisions to your Articles of Organization to include whatever you wish. One of the most popular common extra provisions is the indemnification of managers and members. An indemnification provision states that managers and members aren't personally liable for the company's actions, even if the actions are taken at their own behest. This indemnification provision simply echoes the main point of forming an LLC: the absence of personal liability. Nonetheless, many business owners like to have a formal statement on record making known their intention to take advantage of all indemnities to which they're entitled.

For matters pertaining to how the business is to be run, and for matters that you don't want exposed to the public record, the Operating Agreement will be the principal document of relevance.

| 4 |

The LLC Operating Agreement

Your LLC's *Operating Agreement* details how things are to be done within your LLC. All LLCs should have Operating Agreements, even if there's only one owner. For a single-owner LLC, an Operating Agreement testifies to the owner's seriousness with regard to running the LLC and can be used to defend against creditors' efforts to 'pierce the veil,' rendering the owner personally responsible for debts and legal judgments incurred by the LLC.

One of the unique things about an LLC's Operating Agreement is that it has the ability to supplant (within reasonable bounds) the general cookie-cutter state laws that govern LLCs. This can be a difficult, but critical, process to navigate. As the author of your LLC's Operating Agreement, you have the power to essentially create your own laws that are enforceable in court! If you didn't already retain an attorney when you filed your Articles of Organization, then you should probably get one now.

When written correctly, your Operating Agreement can contribute substantially to the organizational success of your business, from deciding how and when profit shares are to be distributed to determining how disputes are to be resolved within the confines of the LLC. It can be very useful to have an attorney present who can qualify the level of leeway available to the LLC when defining the laws under which you want it to be governed. Attorneys can also be helpful as mediators when the LLC members are negotiating their own various roles within the LLC.

One common mistake new business owners make when forming an LLC is failing to produce an Operating Agreement. The scenario usually looks something like this: you're already drowning in a sea of paperwork with a million and two things to do, you have a well-established personal history with your fellow members, or perhaps even some business experience together, and you think to yourselves, "Operating Agreement? Who's got time for that?"

You must make time. The planning component alone will be advantageous; the time you take together to sit down and think about how things will be done within your company will make it easier for all of the LLC's members to remain on the same page as the business develops. Furthermore, and perhaps most importantly, one of the first things a judge will do in the event of a dispute is look at your Operating Agreement. If every member of the LLC has a clear idea of how things will play out in the event of a dispute, then things should go a lot more smoothly since everyone will know exactly where he or she stands.

Additionally, an operating agreement can protect your business from potentially devastating events. For example, consider a scenario in which one of your LLC's principle owners passes away in an untimely and unexpected way and leaves no will behind. All of his property, including his interest in the LLC, is immediately conferred over to his estranged wife who's always hated the amount of time her husband spent working in the business and hates the people he worked with, including you.

Since you didn't have an operating agreement, state law is the default authority, which mandates that you're forced to accept your deceased partner's wife as a legitimate partner. The very best case scenario here is that the two remaining original partners continue to run the LLC while being forced to give a third of the profits away to someone who's contributing nothing. The alternatives could have catastrophic impacts on the longevity of the business, none of which end well.

Who Does What – Executive Management

The Operating Agreement is where you define rules for your designated managers. Whether your LLC is member-managed or manager-managed, and regardless of whether your managers will soon be known as Chief Marketing Officers or Presidents, those who will be in charge of the most high-level decisions should have their responsibilities spelled out in the Operating Agreement.

An Operating Agreement is Not a Business Plan

When it comes to the content of an Operating Agreement, you're not going to be listing the price of products, the salaries you pay to your secretaries, or the various ways you're going to go about marketing your product, nor will you include a projection of your financials. This is not a business plan. An Operating Agreement speaks primarily to executive relations, profit sharing, divestment, ownership percentages, owner classifications, voting, and so forth.

Business plans are, however, essential planning documents for new businesses of all kinds. If you are building your business from the ground up, check out this resource to guide you: *Business Plan QuickStart Guide*

Operating Agreements for LLCs are typically divided into various provisions. These provisions are like topic headers with each representing a specific dimension of the business. In this chapter we'll review a few common provisions used in Operating Agreements.

The Organization Section

Operating Agreements tend to begin with the Organization Section, which consists of pretty much everything from the Articles of Organization. In fact, you can probably get away with just copying over all the content from the Articles of Organization (see previous chapter).

Note : For an idea of how to organize and present your Operating Agreement, see this website: http://www.techagreements.com/LLC-Operating-Agreements. Aspx. There are more than 100 operating agreements featured here from various industries. You can view their basic structures for free. Viewing any in their entirety may require a fee.

The Membership Interests Section

In this section of the Operating Agreement, the various ownership percentages are defined. Putting together a good Membership Interests section involves a lot more than simply deciding who owns how much. This is where you take into account the various contingencies and unexpected events that, if not planned for, could be disastrous for the business. For example, what happens if a member passes away?

Other things to consider with regard to membership interests include:

- What happens when a member gets divorced? Is that person's spouse entitled to 50% of that person's membership share?

- What happens if a member wants to retire? Does he or she retain all of his interests in the LLC? Is that person forced to divest?

- What happens if one of the LLC's members suddenly stops performing to expectation? Can a majority vote force him or her out of the business?

- What if certain members among the current membership want to bring new members into the LLC? What voting requirements will be necessary? Under what circumstances can existing members be forced to relinquish or sell off their interest?

- Are all members equal, or are there various classifications of members to distinguish various privileges and responsibilities? In your Membership Interest section the identities (including the names and addresses) of the LLC's members must all be specified. You should also include a description of the contributions each member made to the formation of the LLC in the way of cash, material assets, or labor. There should also be a record of the amount of interest (in percentage terms or in terms of shares) conferred upon each member, and if you're dividing your membership into classes, then you need to specify the class category next to each member. Have every member of the LLC sign his or her name next to this data.

When it comes to assigning various classifications to members, the most common distinction many LLCs make is voting rights. Some shares of the LLC come with the right to vote, and thereby affect the business's executive level decisions, while others offer no such privilege.

A few things to remember about voting rights:

- You needn't issue specific voting right and non-voting right shares immediately; you can reserve the right to issue voting shares at a later time.

- It's perfectly fine for members to hold both voting and non-voting shares of the LLC.

Your Membership Interest section should also include details on how the LLC will accommodate new ownership interests—members who come in later. Think of a law firm for example. Most law firms award hard working attorneys after years of service by making them partners in the firm. Many law firms operate as *professional service LLCs* and probably have their new member procedures down in writing in their Operating Agreements.

Consider these when drawing up regulations governing new members:

- Should the new members be required to 'buy-in,' by contributing money, service or equipment?

  Note : When a new member contributes money, equipment, services or other assets to the LLC in exchange for membership interest, the IRS does not see it as a gain or a loss for the new member or the LLC but an exchange of equal value. Similar to the transition of money from one account to another, it's not taxed.

- How will you determine the real value of what you're giving away? In other words, if you're issuing a membership interest to a new party, then it's usually prudent to figure out how much the membership shares are worth at the time of issuance. That way, if you are taking contributions from the new member in exchange for her membership interests, you will be able to scale the value.

- Voting-wise, what does it take to bring a new member into the fold? Some LLCs are ok with a simple majority, while others don't want new members unless there is unanimous approval within the existing membership.

  Note : On the matter of profit-shares for new members, the most common way of handling this issue is to give the new member his or her profit percentage on the basis of what percentage of the LLC he or she now owns and when that person received his or her membership shares in relation to the fiscal year.

  Ex: if Sharon, a new member, is given a 10% ownership in the company on the first day of the final quarter of the fiscal year, then she will receive only 25% of her 10% entitlement when distributions are made at the end of the fiscal calendar.

Q1 25% of 10%	Q2 25% of 10%	100% of Sharon's 10% Stake
Q3 25% of 10%	Q4 25% of 10%	Q1 + Q2 + Q3 + Q4 = 100%

On the matter of how ownership shares in the LLC can be bought, sold, assigned, or transferred, if there's more than one set of rules in play for various members or according to the various classifications of membership, then a separate buy-sell agreement should be written out for each member or member class. The buy-sell agreement, or what may be referred to as "buy-sell provisions," may be incorporated in the Operating Agreement (putting it in the Membership Interest section is fine) or it may exist independently, though it must be signed by all members and filed with the rest of the LLC paperwork.

Note : Assignment is the legal transfer of rights from one person (the assignor) to another (the assignee). The term encompasses nearly all legal transfers of rights such as that of duties and obligations, ownership, rights (such as the right to vote or the right to receive profit), and any contractual benefits.

While legal assignment doesn't need to be explicitly written (it only must show intent to transfer) no one will advise that your contracts be verbal. Assignment— especially when changing share values, voting rights, and ownership are involved—can get pretty complex. It's best to consult an experienced business lawyer when hashing out the particulars of important assignments.

The bottom line is that you definitely need a buy-sell agreement if you want to avoid some very uncomfortable scenarios. For example, consider the fictional plight of Mary, Rachel and Steve, who opened a gym together and used an LLC to safeguard themselves from personal liabilities. Three years into the business Mary cannot stand the sight of Steve, Mary and Rachel are constantly at odds with one another over key business decisions, and the whole business has become very dysfunctional.

To make matters worse, Mary is dying to get out of the gym business and open a vitamin/nutrition shop, and theoretically, if she were to sell her interest in the gym business, she'd have enough money to get the ball rolling on her new endeavor. She's more than willing to sell her interest in the company, the only problem is that no one can clearly determine or agree on exactly how much her share is worth.

They didn't include any buy-sell provisions to detail how share values were to be determined, so Mary's notion of how much she's entitled to is vastly higher than what Steve and Rachel think is reasonable. There's no way out.

When it comes to exiting the LLC, there are two scenarios to consider:

Scenario 1 :   The other LLC members purchase the departing member's interest

Scenario 2 :   The departing member sells her interest to a third party. Without a detailed buy-sell agreement (or buy-sell provisions) clearly in place, this process can become very difficult.

When the LLC buys back its shares from a departing member, the ownership percentages are reconfigured. If there were originally five partners, each owning 20%, and one partner departs, then after the LLC buys back its shares, the remaining four owners will each own 25%. In regards to how the value of the LLC is to be assessed and translated into a hard dollar amount, various states have different laws that dictate how these valuations and transactions are to take place. If you do not have a buy-sell agreement in writing, then you and your partners are at the mercy of the state's laws, which may not always be a good thing for your business or your business interests.

Usually shares of an LLC are not sold to parties outside of the LLC until the parties *inside* the LLC have first been given a chance to purchase the shares for themselves. This is known as 'the right of first refusal.' If no current members of the LLC want to purchase a departing member's shares, then they can then be sold to the public at-large. When a person or entity outside the LLC buys into it, he or she will not automatically have voting rights inside the LLC, only a guaranteed share of the profits and losses. Existing members must first authorize voting rights for the new party.

The Allocations & Distributions Section

It's important to understand the difference between profit/loss allocations and profit distributions in an LLC. *Allocations* are usually based on a member's percentage share in the LLC. If John owns 50% of an LLC, he is usually entitled to a 50% allocation of the LLC's profit and loss. Furthermore, John will be taxed on any profit that results from this allocation, even if the profit isn't distributed to him. *Distributions* refer to the actual remitting of cash to members of the LLC.

Distributions may or may not be issued in accordance with the LLC's established allocations. Often, especially during the early years, members prefer to put money back into the business rather than take their distributions. Such elections result in the problem of *phantom income*, whereby members are taxed on monies they didn't even receive. Taxes on LLCs follow allocations, not distributions. Be sure to keep this in mind when creating the Allocations and Distributions section of your LLC's Operating Agreement. Also be sure to include a description of what happens to departing or newly-arriving members in terms of allocation and distribution amounts. The most common way to handle this is by simply pro-rating their entitlements according to the fiscal calendar.

The Meeting & Voting Section

LLCs are given a lot more leeway than corporations when it comes to how high-level meetings are organized and how frequently they're held. Corporations are bound by law to a certain schedule, whereas the rules governing an LLC can be set forth autonomously in the LLC's Operating Agreement.

Distribution

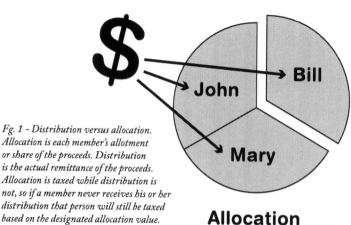

Fg. 1 - Distribution versus allocation. Allocation is each member's allotment or share of the proceeds. Distribution is the actual remittance of the proceeds. Allocation is taxed while distribution is not, so if a member never receives his or her distribution that person will still be taxed based on the designated allocation value.

Allocation

Considerations about your LLC's meeting & voting practices:

- How much voting power should be wielded by the various members, and on what basis? The most common way to determine voting power in an LLC is to make it directly proportionate to the membership shares. If a person owns 75% of the LLC, then that person controls 75% of the vote. Some LLCs give every member an equal vote, regardless of ownership percentage.

- What types of decisions will require a vote? Common vote-worthy decisions include whether or not the LLC should sell property, whether the LLC should change the Operating Agreement, whether key responsibilities should be transferred, or if different individuals should be appointed to key officer positions within the LLC. Depending on the gravity of the decision at-hand, a majority vote or a unanimous vote may be required. Examples of scenarios in which a unanimous vote may be appropriate include: selling the business, making a major investment, or resolving a lawsuit through a substantial settlement.

- How must notice be given before a meeting is held? It's a good idea to specify this in your Operating Agreement. Specifying notice requirements can preemptively diffuse scenarios in which members purposefully obfuscate meeting details to prevent other members from who may threaten their agendas from attending.

- Should the LLC establish a quorum? A quorum refers to the number of members that need to be present in order for a meeting to take place. An LLC may elect not to conduct any business in a meeting without unanimous attendance, or it may stipulate that a majority or certain percentage is sufficient. When considering this piece of your meeting and voting section, keep in mind that getting autonomous owner/partners to show up for meetings is oftentimes easier said than done. Make sure that you don't hinder the flow of business by making your meeting requirements too stringent.

- Can members vote by proxy? To avoid ambiguity, be sure to specify whether or not members can vote in ways other than in person. You should also specify the extent to which members may participate in voting by way of telephone, video conference, or other means.

If you are truly stumped when it comes to meetings, votes, or any group decisions, there is a variety of literature available on the subject. Known as parliamentary procedure, the process of creating a structure for meetings of the assembly can be very useful in creating a fair and orderly discussion and decision-making environment. One of the most popular and venerated systems is Robert's Rules of Order, so to learn more check out our handy guide to success: *Roberts Rules QuickStart Guide.*

Manager Responsibility & Authority

If you're setting up a manager-managed LLC, then you're going to be imbuing a person (or organization) with a high degree of autonomy over your business. The responsibilities and limits placed upon your manager should be clarified in your Operating Agreement. You should include information on how this person (or entity) is to be compensated, the scope of the agreements that he can make on behalf of the LLC, his ability to hire and fire employees, and his ability to buy and sell assets on behalf of the company.

In this section, it's also very important to include procedures for how the LLC's management is selected as well as the level of job security that they're offered. For example, you may want to guarantee a manager a two-year tenure at the business and then, at that point, have the members vote on whether to reinstate the manager or let him go.

Managers of LLCs are able to make agreements and enter into contracts on behalf of the company. Even if the manager exceeds the limits explicitly stated in the Operating Agreement, the LLC is still responsible for all contracts entered into and debts acquired by the manager. Such contracts can only be voided at a judge's discretion, which means that it is extremely important to lay down the constraints under which a manager may operate.

Other Potential Provisions

Your LLC's Operating Agreement is where you establish the law of the land for your business. You're free to include anything you want, within reason, to set forth how your business will operate. You can include provisions on how, where and by whom records will be kept in your company. You can specify how you wish dispute resolution to take place within the confines of the company. Perhaps most importantly, you should specify how dissolution of the LLC could and would take place. What events will trigger dissolution? Who gets paid first after all of the company's debts are settled?

Get it Signed

Making sure all the LLC's members sign the Operating Agreement is a lot more than just a formality. It is imperative to making the Operating Agreement binding and enforceable. Failing to have all members sign can and does create serious, preventable legal expenditures down the road should one or more of your members claim that he or she never agreed to the terms that you worked so hard to establish in your Operating Agreement.

To make the Operating Agreement and all its provisions ironclad, all LLC members should verify with their signatures all of their capital contributions and their membership interests. Hold a meeting with all member parties present in which the Operating Agreement is voted upon and approved. Note the event in the meeting minutes and have all members sign the minutes to prove they were there.

Congratulations, your Operating Agreement is now ironclad and court enforceable!

| 5 |

Understanding Your Tax Options

With pass-through taxation, single-owner LLCs are essentially taxed as sole proprietorships and multi-owner LLCs are taxed as partnerships. In both cases, the entity itself is not taxed independently, as it would be in the case of a corporation, but the profits generated are taxed as individual income received by the owners. LLCs, as was mentioned previously in this book, also can elect to be taxed as corporations.

Things don't really get complicated until you start to consider the differences between allocations and distributions for tax purposes. Allocations and distributions were reviewed in the previous chapter, and thorough definitions for each term are available in the glossary at the end of this book. It is the LLC member's allocation—not distribution—amount that determines how much he or she is taxed.

Distributions are how much that individual received in cash from the company as a share of profit. As previously stated, LLCs are at liberty to distribute however they see fit in accordance with their Operating Agreements. They are not free, however, to pay their taxes whenever they choose.

So, things can get complicated. What if after five years of operation a company finds itself flush with cash and wants to provide its members with a hefty windfall? The members have been taxed over the previous five years in accordance with their allocations, so how do the owners know exactly how much tax they have to pay on the windfall? The answer lies in the use of a concept called a *tax basis.*

Every member of an LLC has a tax basis, which simply refers to a tracking process that quantifies how much the owner has currently paid in taxes, regardless of how much money has been distributed to that person. The concept of phantom income refers to an LLC member's accrual of a payable tax liability, even if he or she has not yet received the money that's being taxed. The owner's tax basis determines how much of the LLC's profits are *not* taxable, either because they've already been taxed or because they're offsetting valid losses or expenditures and are therefore not really profits.

When the LLC distributes profits to its owners, each of them will subtract the amount on which that person has already been taxed (the tax basis), and then will pay tax only on the remainder amount. An owner's tax basis is increased when he or she contributes money, property, or any other capital expenditure to the business. When the business turns a profit and these profits <u>are allocated</u> (not necessarily paid) to the members, then the members' tax bases go up. If a loss is reported and allocated to the members, then their tax bases go down.

The bases also go down when the LLC distributes cash or property to the owners. The basis cannot go below zero, even in the event that a downward adjustment to the basis theoretically reduces the basis to a number below zero. The basis would simply remain at zero in this circumstance.

> *Note : A negative tax base technically means that the government owes the LLC member money rather than the other way around, therefore, activity that produces a negative tax base only reduces the number to zero—never below.*

The main purpose of these basis adjustment rules is to help the LLC keep track of which profits can be distributed tax-free (because they've already been taxed, technically) and which profits need to be taxed before they're distributed. If this explanation seems convoluted, consider the following scenario to see basis adjustment in action.

Business partners Stan and Mark decide they're going to open a deli in New York City called East Side Meats. To protect their personal assets, they form an LLC in which both Stan and Mark have 50%

interest. Stan and Mark each contribute $20,000 to get the store up and running. After their first year in business, the deli turns a net profit of $80,000. The net profit is allocated (not distributed) equally between the partners at $40,000 each, and, since an LLC is taxed by default as a partnership, pass-through taxation applies—remember that LLCs that are not taxed as corporations are considered disregarded entities. Both Stan and Mark must pay taxes on $40,000 as if it were a part of their regular self-employment incomes. In order to make sure that the owners of East Side Meats always have cash on hand to deal with their tax burden, a provision was written into their Operating Agreement that states "members are to receive distribution of 40% of allocated net profits after each year." This provision forces the LLC to at least pay Stan and Mark enough to pay their taxes. So after year one, both Stan and Mark receive a distribution of $16,000 each from the LLC which is, as per the Operating Agreement, 40% of their allocated net profits.

At this point, the partners pay their taxes for the year and the tax basis for both partners is now at $24,000 ($40,000-$16,000), because they both have $24,000 that hasn't been distributed but has been taxed. If the following year the business earns $100,000 in profit, allocated at $50,000 a piece between the partners, then the LLC's total cash on-hand (including cash retained from the previous year) would be $148,000. Here's where keeping track of the tax basis for each owner on an ongoing basis comes in handy. We know that some of the $148,000 in the LLC's account has already been taxed, but how much?

Let's say the LLC decides to pay it back to the owners, $74,000 a piece to both Stan and Mark. Begin with Stan or Mark's tax basis from the previous year: $24,000. The $74,000 distribution would cause the basis to go down to zero (it can't go below), leaving $50,000 ($74,000-$24,000 = $50,000) of income that's taxable in the second year. When the proper tax basis is maintained for each member, it's always clear who owes what and when.

East Side Deli – Year 1

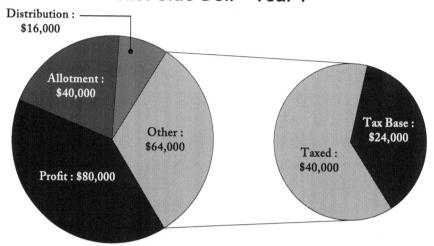

Fg. 2 - The allotment, distribution, and taxation breakdown for the East Side Deli for its first year of operation. Note that the entire allotment was taxed, even though each member only received $16,000. This creates a tax base of $24,000 (income that was taxed but never received).

East Side Deli – Year 1

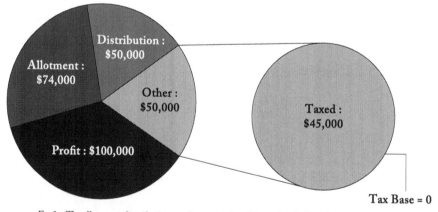

Fg. 3 - The allotment, distribution, and taxation breakdown for the East Side Deli for its second year of operation. Note that the $24,000 tax base was applied to the taxable allotment, reducing it to zero. In this instance, the reduction in tax base meant that the allotment and distribution were equal, and each member paid taxes on the money that he actually received.

IRS Paperwork

The IRS paperwork required for filing taxes for your LLC depends on how you elect to be taxed. Single-member LLCs still file as if they were sole proprietorships, using a schedule C form and attaching it to their 1040 personal income tax returns.

If you have a multi-member LLC and it's being taxed as a partnership (as it will be by default unless you petition the IRS to be taxed differently), then you will fill out a Form 1065. The 1065 isn't a return but a notice to the IRS that gives information about your LLC, and, most importantly, defines the tax allocations among your members.

There are certain sections on your Form 1065 that can have significant tax ramifications for all members, such as whether or not you qualify for a research credit and the extent to which your assets have depreciated. Each of these sections should be reviewed with deference to what's specified in the LLC's Operating Agreement, or taken to a meeting and agreed upon collectively by the membership as they will all be affected by the outcome. You may also want to seek the advice of an accountant.

All members of the LLC receive a Schedule K-1 from the LLC's accountant or whoever is preparing the LLC's taxes. Allocations of company income for each member are clarified on the Schedule K-1, as are the member's capital contributions to the LLC, which can be written off as deductions.

Note : The Schedule K-1 is more complicated than it seems, as various income and expenditure types, such as short and long-term capital gains, rental real estate income, charitable contributions, royalties and other categories, must be delineated on the form. Take a look over the form and if it seems a bit overwhelming, get an accountant involved.

To report income from the LLC, members should file a schedule E, which is technically used to report income derived from sources outside the taxpayer's primary income source. If the LLC is the main way that you're generating income for yourself, then you should add yourself to the LLC's payroll and pay your standard payroll tax. Reserve the schedule E for the allocation earnings that are generated from the LLC. These earnings are considered secondary income.

In the introduction to this book we talked about filing Form 8832 (Entity Classification Election) to have your LLC taxed as a corporation. Basically, the corporation is treated as if it were a completely separate entity subject to its own direct taxation and responsible for filing its own income tax return. The form used is Form 1120: US Corporation Income Tax Return, and you'll actually send this form at the same time as your Form 8832. Corporate profits are subject to the federal corporate tax, which is approximately 15 percent. The major drawback to being taxed as a corporation is the potential to have profits double taxed, first in the form of the corporate tax, then as capital gains when the corporation's earnings are distributed to the shareholders.

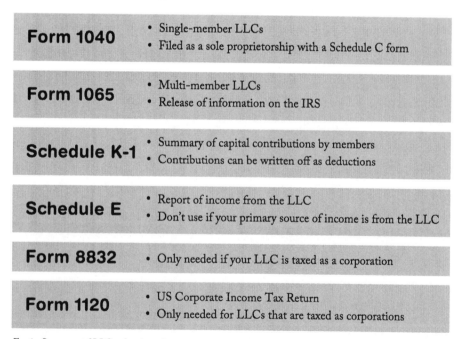

Form 1040
- Single-member LLCs
- Filed as a sole proprietorship with a Schedule C form

Form 1065
- Multi-member LLCs
- Release of information on the IRS

Schedule K-1
- Summary of capital contributions by members
- Contributions can be written off as deductions

Schedule E
- Report of income from the LLC
- Don't use if your primary source of income is from the LLC

Form 8832
- Only needed if your LLC is taxed as a corporation

Form 1120
- US Corporate Income Tax Return
- Only needed for LLCs that are taxed as corporations

Fg. 4 - Summary of LLC-related tax forms.

| 6 |

Choosing the Right State

It's not uncommon for an LLC to be based in a state separate from the owner's home state (foreign operation). This is perfectly legal and may lead to an optimal business strategy for you and the other members of your LLC.

As was mentioned in the Introduction to this book, different states have different laws when it comes to governing LLCs. If a particular state's laws really appeal to you and you want to form your LLC there but do business in another state (such as your own), be forewarned. As a business owner, you can form your LLC anywhere, but if you're planning to do business somewhere else, you will be subject to the laws, taxes, and disclosure requirements of the state in which you transact business. In fact, on order for an LLC to do any business outside of the state in which it was formed, it must register to transact business in the alternate location. This is known as qualifying or foreign filing.

For Conventional, Brick-and-Mortar Storefronts

If you're going to be doing business from a traditional, geographically-fixed location, such as a dental practice or a bakery, then you're better off forming your LLC in the state where it will ultimately operate. Otherwise you will still be required to register to transact business in the state in which you plan to operate, and you will just waste time and money trying to file elsewhere. If you're going to be operating in multiple states, then you will need to register to transact business in all the states in which you'll be operating.

One of the few exceptions to this general rule for brick-and-mortars comes into effect if you happen to live in a state where the type of LLC you want to form is not permitted. For example, some states don't allow the formation of single-member LLCs, and some don't have options for professional services LLCs. Your only option at this point is to form your LLC in a state where your chosen format is permitted, then register to transact business in the state in which you live.

For Non-Conventional Businesses

If you're not going to set up a traditional brick-and-mortar storefront, but operate your business online or in some other non-centralized way, then it will be a good use of your time to look for a state that is very business-friendly to LLCs. Many states want to host this type of business and have worked to establish an environment that will attract companies who have geographic flexibility.

| 7 |

How to Convert into an LLC

Maybe, after reading this book, you've decided that you'd better jump on this LLC bandwagon before your sole proprietorship or partnership gets into trouble and suddenly your kid's college fund goes up in smoke. In this chapter, we'll explain how you can transition your existing business into an LLC—where permitted by state law.

Converting From a Sole Proprietorship

If you'd like to turn your sole proprietorship into a single-member LLC, then you're in luck as far as effort is concerned. The process is quite straight-forward. Since all of your business assets are already officially in your own name, you simply transfer them to your LLC in exchange for your membership interest in your LLC. As previously mentioned, most states will allow the formation of single-member LLCs, though there are some exceptions.

In the event that you must have at least one partner to form an LLC, and assuming moving to a different state to file doesn't make sense, then consider getting a minority partner, a friend or a relative, who will own 2-4% of the LLC. You're not required to distribute any profits to this person if you don't wish to do so. He or she can just play the role of a silent partner and allow you to qualify for some of the advantages of having a multi-partner LLC that wouldn't have been available to you as a single owner.

When you transfer your assets into the LLC, it is considered a non-taxable event, which is a good thing, as you will not be taxed on the value of your sole proprietorship's assets. The only tricky thing with this transfer, tax-wise, is the transfer of what's known as *recourse debt*, which is business debt for which the owner is personally liable. Once you convert that debt into the LLC, it will be shielded, therefore the IRS wants you to pay taxes on it. They treat this debt transfer as a deemed cash distribution. If your sole proprietorship has business liabilities that you have personally guaranteed, then the value of those liabilities will be taxed when you form the LLC. If you fear that this deemed cash distribution is going to create a particularly heavy tax burden for you, then seek out the services of a professional accountant. They have ways of helping you minimize or completely bypass this type of scenario.

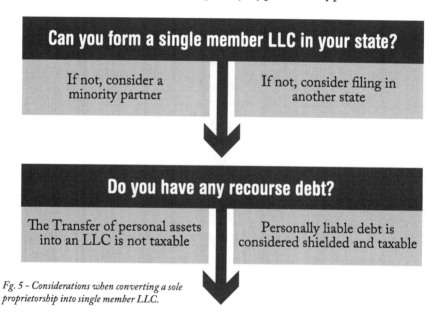

Can you form a single member LLC in your state?

| If not, consider a minority partner | If not, consider filing in another state |

Do you have any recourse debt?

| The Transfer of personal assets into an LLC is not taxable | Personally liable debt is considered shielded and taxable |

Fg. 5 - Considerations when converting a sole proprietorship into single member LLC.

Converting From a Partnership

Converting to an LLC from a partnership is also incredibly simple, mainly because LLCs and partnerships have identical tax structures. The only key difference is that with the LLC you and your partners will be protected from personal liability.

Just as with the sole proprietorship conversion, when converting from a partnership to an LLC, all partners transfer the business assets they own into the LLC in exchange for membership. You will, of course, need all of the partners to agree to make the conversion before proceeding. This transfer of assets is tax-free.

Be careful when transferring over any personally guaranteed recourse debt to the newly formed LLC. Just as with the sole proprietorship conversions, the IRS may deem this transfer as a taxable cash distribution.

Converting From a Corporation

While corporations provide liability protection and are useful for raising capital from outside investors, they can create tax trouble for growing businesses that see both their corporation's profits taxed twice, first when it is initially made, and then again after it is distributed. According to section 721 of the Internal Revenue Code, corporations can transfer property to an LLC without paying any taxes on it, just like an individual can. Any assets your corporation holds that have appreciated over time will not be taxed according to the increase in their value. These assets will be seen as having retained their original value and will only be taxable when they're sold back into the market.

Things can get really complicated when transferring corporate assets into an LLC. The federal paperwork is complicated enough, and if you manage to get through it, you'll still have to tackle the state and local paperwork, which may include unforeseen tax requirements. It may be less costly to process your conversion as a merger with the LLC as the surviving entity, or you may be better off pursuing a "statutory conversion," which converts a corporation into an LLC without legally dissolving it first.

Some corporations also discover that a *dual-entity* strategy fits their needs best, whereby both the corporation and the LLC continue to exist, and the LLC simply leases assets from the corporation to undertake its operations. To explore these many options within the context of all applicable laws, you're best off enlisting the services of a qualified accountant.

If converting to an LLC or a corporation doesn't fit the needs of your business today, don't disregard the value that restructuring can have. The question 'should we change our status?' should be frequently revisited as the needs of your business change. The marketplace is a dynamic force; what doesn't work today, may be a necessity tomorrow.

| 8 |

Knowing When Not to Form an LLC

So far, we have spent a lot of time discussing the many positives of LLCs, and that's not incorrect; LLCs have been ideal for many businesses. They do have limitations, however, and what works for one business or industry may not be a good fit for another. This chapter focuses on arming you with the knowledge necessary to make an informed decision regarding whether the LLC structure is best for you. We'll be discussing alternative structures so let's start with a review of the business entity classifications available.

C Corporation	The business entity is subject to federal income tax, and shareholders are not subject to tax unless they collect dividends, distributions, or salary.
S Corporation	The business entity is *not* subject to federal income tax, though the company's shareholders pay federal income tax on the taxable portion of the company's profits.
LLC	Like S Corporations, LLCs are pass-through entities (unless they elect to be taxed as corporations). LLCs are effectively sole proprietorships for tax reasons (or partnerships in the case of multi-member LLCs) with a legal shield.
Sole Proprietorship/ Partnership	These are easy and cheaply established. They offer no liability protection, and profits are considered taxable personal income.

Is Your LLC Investor Friendly?

The short answer is 'no, probably not'. Even though you may have a booming business with plans to expand (hence the need for serious investors) or a killer product that will revolutionize the industry (hence the need for serious investors), the LLC format can put up roadblocks for serious investors. These roadblocks are particularly pronounced in the tech and startup sectors in which companies may go through multiple massive rounds of financing and reinvestment.

Many Investors Simply Don't Like LLCs

Don't take it personally, but many investors prefer to stay away from entity-based taxation. This can complicate their tax situation and can result in them being taxed on allocations for which they never receive distributions. Additionally, many investors like 'easy in, easy out' investments, and because LLCs are contractually constructed—as opposed to constructed based on statutes, as is the case with corporations—each investment scenario may be radically different based on the Operating Agreements of various LLCs.

Not only do some investors simply not like LLCs, but some can't invest in LLCs. Venture funds are particularly unable to invest in LLCs or other pass-through entities because they often have tax-exempt partners. Pass-through taxation means that if an exempt partner has a stake in an LLC, then that entity (it may not just be a person) is subject to taxes and may jeopardize its exemption status.

Successful investors have turned their investment practices into a science, if not an art. They understand that to optimize their investments they must consistently reinvest in the businesses in their portfolio. The Operating Agreements of many LLCs have provisions that state when profits will be distributed, how much will be distributed, and how much will remain in the business. Circumstances like this can hamper effective investor reinvestment and can be detrimental to a healthy and profitable investment.

Even if all of the aforementioned aspects weren't present with LLCs, the bottom line is that many investors may not be as familiar with their structure and operation as they are with traditional corporations that have been around for significantly longer. Remember that LLCs are relative newcomers to the business entity playing field and as a result have much less uniform structure. Investments are, in many cases, controlled wagers, and when placing a wager, it is better to stick with what you know rather than throw money at something you don't understand.

Together, all of these characteristics mean that LLCs are often poor candidates for professional and serious investors. While it is possible to write your Operating Agreement in a way that makes your LLC more attractive to investors, many will pass it over without a second glance. This is not to say that you can't secure effective investment for your LLC, just be aware that many investors are less than motivated to part with their capital for LLCs.

Taxation for LLCs Can be Complicated

We know that venture firms with exempt partners will stay away from pass-through entities, but the tax implications don't end there. If an investor is not dissuaded by all of the aforementioned complications, there is still the potential exposure to tax liability in multiple states.

Let's say that a passive investor in New York has a friend in California. Mr. New York invests a large amount in Mr. California's food truck business, The Beach Ball Shrimp Truck LLC. Even as a passive investor, Mr. New York will receive a Form K-1 from California and have to file an income tax return with the state of California.

Remember, allotment is taxed, not distribution, so Mr. New York could owe taxes on his share of the company without seeing a return on his investment. Professional investors make their living by reaping the benefits of their investments; do you think that paying taxes on 'phantom income' is appealing to these kinds of people? Not only do foreign investors (from another state) expose themselves to multi-state tax liability, but the same kind of thing happens to alien investors—investors from outside the US.

The complexity of LLC taxation in conjunction with the other roadblocks for investors means that the simplicity of owning stock in a traditional C Corp is much more attractive, especially when the business is at an early stage. The exchange is pretty simple: the investor or investing entity acquires the capital asset (stock) and then records a capital gain/loss event when the stock is sold.

When investing in C Corps there is no potential for multiple state taxation, and the sale of the stock is predictable – a simple transaction that it is structured through regulation. LLCs, on the other hand, are often governed by complicated Operating Agreements and other contracts. This means that the sale of ownership within the company could potentially be different with each different company and that there are a lot more variables to manage.

Keeping within the tax implications and investment barriers associated with LLCs, raising capital comes with its own set of challenges. Let's say that you have overcome the hesitance that many investors have with investing in LLCs and you now have a reliable pool of investors. With a C Corp, there are structures in place that simplify raising various rounds of capital. No such structures exist for LLCs, and at the very least, your investors are stuck with tax obligations on their investments the very next year.

Concerns for Members

Stepping away from the issues that LLCs present to investors, let's take a look at the complications that LLCs present to members—

both single-member and multi-member LLCs. While LLCs can offer substantial advantages over the traditional sole proprietorship entity structure, those advantages do come with a cost.

As we have covered time and time again, LLCs are built with contracts to a much greater extent than they are built with statutes. Sometimes referred to as 'contract creatures' (as opposed to 'statutory creatures' such as corporations) LLCs have a lot of variability and complexity. This means that the free form nature of LLCs must be structured and tethered with contracts. These contracts are of the utmost importance to the organization and, as a result, can be complex, costly, and difficult to assemble.

While the underlying advantage that this confers—the ability to shape the organization how you see fit—is a versatile tool, getting the details wrong can have a profoundly negative effect later on down the road. This is something of a liability for members and for the organization at large, but it also serves to dissuade investors.

As was covered earlier in this chapter, investors are wary of investing in contract creatures like LLCs, as their modes of operation can vary wildly from company to company.

Equity compensation is also more difficult in LLCs that are taxed as partnerships. Due to the lack of statutory guidelines regarding equity compensation within LLCs, the process becomes complicated and time consuming as LLCs are forced to 'book up' or adjust capital accounts for each instance of equity sharing.

If it isn't immediately obvious to you which entity structure you should choose—and even if it is—a consultation with a CPA is in order. A tax and business professional can give you the expertise and advice you need to make an informed decision regarding which entity structure is in your best interest. You can also find additional information about each entity in our Accounting and Tax sections

conclusion

Every business owner should understand the types of protections an LLC offers, especially if the business owner has a significant pool of personal assets that could be taken away as the result of one bad judgment or a failed business with debts. The time and expense requirements to form an LLC are negligible when compared to the value of what the LLC can protect.

When deciding whether to form an LLC, it's of paramount importance that you consider your exit strategy for your business as well as the options you wish to have available for capital. Corporations offer the same type of liability protection and most investors and venture capitalists prefer them. The structure and operational norms of a corporation are also clearer, as they've been around for centuries and have been described and refined with an abundance of case law.

Finally, know your state-by-state rules that govern LLCs. There is much similarity state-by-state when it comes to LLC formation, but what you don't know can hurt you. State-specific professional help is available in the form of an attorney or a formation company.

You can also use sites that provide a run-down on state-by-state variance like this:

http://www.nolo.com/legal-encyclopedia/form-llc-in-your-state-31019.html

glossary

Allocations-
Since LLC's aren't taxed as independent entities, the owners of the LLC are subject to pass-through taxation, and the LLCs earnings are taxed through the owners' personal tax incomes. Allocations simply refer to the amount of an LLC's earnings or loss attributed to the members within the LLC.

Articles of Organization-
Formal documentation filed with the state- usually at the Secretary of State's office—that brings an LLC into legal formation.

Corporation-
A business entity that exists and can be taxed wholly independently from its owners and shareholders. This is distinct from an LLC, which isn't treated as a separate taxable entity by default.

C Corporation-
The standard legal form of a corporation, named for Subchapter C of the IRS tax code.

Distributions-
In the context of LLCs, distributions refer to profits that are given to the LLC's members in the form of cash or some other asset. Distributions are separate from allocations. An LLC owner, through the allocation of profits that the LLC earns, may be allocated a portion of profits on which he must pay taxes, but this does not necessarily mean that he receives the same amount in distributions. See "Phantom Income."

DBA (Doing Business As)-
A fictitious name or trade name used by businesses, usually sole proprietors or partnerships, that operate under a name that's not their legal name.

Disregarded Entity-
An entity that is not taxed directly, usually because the owner claims any taxable profits the entity achieves through allocations. The owners of the entity then pay the required tax on their personal tax returns. See 'Pass-through Taxation.'

Dual Entity Strategy-
A strategy employed by a corporation seeking to convert into an LLC, whereby the corporation remains legally existent and the LLC leases the corporation's assets for operational use.

Dual Protection-
A unique feature of an LLC, whereby not only are the members limited in their personal liability for the actions of the company, but the company is also immune from the personal actions of its members. If a member of an LLC acquires a personal liability— such as a judgment against him in a lawsuit—his shares of the LLC cannot be confiscated, even if he has nothing else available to confiscate.

Formation Company-
Companies that specialize in creating (forming) LLCs and other business entities, usually offering their services for a significant discount relative to what one would pay an attorney for similar services.

Form 8832-
The form that must be filed when an LLC elects to be taxed as a corporation.

LLC (Limited Liability Company)-
A relatively new type of business entity that's characterized by pass-through taxation and protecting its members' personal assets from liability hazards common in business.

Manager-Managed-
A type of management arrangement in which the LLC partners elect or hire a manager to conduct affairs on behalf of the business. The manager may or may not be a member of the LLC.

Member-Managed-
A type of management arrangement in which the LLC partners manage the business on their own through voting and designating various member responsibilities for the business's executive functioning.

Operating Agreement-
A legally binding document that defines ownership roles, responsibilities, authorizations, and profit-shares in an LLC.

Partnership-
Two or more individuals who go into business together. Members of a partnership may be personally liable for the debts and legal judgments (liabilities) incurred against the business.

Pass-through Taxation-
A system wherby a business entity is not taxed independently, but the business entity's profits are allocated and taxed on the business's owners' individual tax returns.

Phantom Income-
A phenomenon that occurs when a member of an LLC is taxed on income that was never distributed. If, for example, a two-member LLC achieves $500,000 in profits one year, $400,000 is invested back into the business, and only $100,000 is distributed equally among the two partners, $50,000 apiece. Each partner will still have a tax liability of $250,000, even though he or she only received $50,000 in distributions.

Professional Service LLC-
LLCs available in some states that are specifically designed for groups of licensed professionals such as accountants, doctors, dentists, lawyers, or engineers. Professional service LLCs often aren't guaranteed as much insulation from personal liability as standard LLCs.

Registered Agent-
In an LLC's Article of Organizations, registered agents are named and these individuals essentially personify the LLC, acting as its ambassador to the outside world. An LLC that's being sued, for example, is considered to be formally served with legal paperwork once the LLC's registered agent is served.

S Corporation-
A type of tax filing available for
corporations that subject them to
tax governance under Subchapter S
of the IRS tax code. The members
of an S Corporation are subject to
pass-through taxation as opposed
to having the corporation taxed
as an independent entity.

Self-Employment Tax-
The combination of Social Security and
Medicare taxes levied on individuals
who receive certain types of income
– such as LLC business profits. These
taxes are higher than the Social
Security and Medicare taxes paid
by wage earners, because the self-
employed individual is paying both
his half of the obligation as well as the
half normally paid by an employer.

Sole Proprietorship-
When an individual goes into business,
the business is considered a sole
proprietorship. It's the simplest type of
business to form, but the individual's
personal assets are at risk for any
liabilities incurred by the company.

Tax Basis-
In the context of LLCs, the tax basis
is a type of ledger that provides a way
of keeping track of tax liabilities in the
business when distributions vary from
year to year, often disproportionate
to the business's allocations.

about clydebank

We are a multi-media publishing company that provides reliable, high-quality and easily accessible information to a global customer base. Developed out of the need for beginner-friendly content that is accessible across multiple formats, we deliver reliable, up-to-date, high-quality information through our multiple product offerings.

Through our strategic partnerships with some of the world's largest retailers, we are able to simplify the learning process for customers around the world, providing them with an authoritative source of information for the subjects that matter to them. Our end-user focused philosophy puts the satisfaction of our customers at the forefront of our mission. We are committed to creating multi-media products that allow our customers to learn what they want, when they want and how they want.

ClydeBank Business is a division of the multimedia-publishing firm ClydeBank Media LLC. ClydeBank Media's goal is to provide affordable, accessible information to a global market through different forms of media such as eBooks, paperback books and audio books. Company divisions are based on subject matter, each consisting of a dedicated team of researchers, writers, editors and designers.

For more information, please visit us at :
www.clydebankmedia.com
or contact *info@clydebankmedia.com*

Your world, simplified.

notes

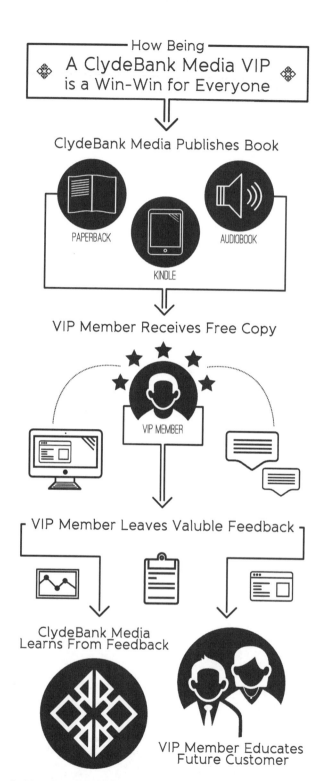

Visit *www.clydebankmedia.com/vip* to find out more and become a VIP member!

Get a *FREE* ClydeBank Media Audiobook + 30 Day Free Trial to Audible.com

Get titles like this absolutely free :

- *Business Plan Quickstart Guide*
- *Options Trading Quickstart Guide*
- *ITIL Quickstart Guide*
- *Scrum Quickstart Guide*
- *JavaScript Quickstart Guide*
- *3D Printing Quickstart Guide*

- *LLC Quickstart Guide*
- *Lean Six Sigma Quickstart Guide*
- *Project Management QuickStart Guide*
- *Social Security Simplified*
- *Medicare Simplified*
- *and more!*

To Sign Up & Get your Free Audiobook, visit :
www.clydebankmedia.com/audible-trial

Made in the USA
Middletown, DE
23 April 2016